ARTWORK PROVIDED BY FREEDESIGNFILE.COM

ARTWORK PROVIDED BY FREEDESIGNFILE.COM

ARTWORK PROVIDED BY FREEDESIGNFILE.COM

ARTWORK PROVIDED BY FREEDESIGNFILE.COM

www.ingramcontent.com/pod-product-compliance
Lightning Source LLC
Chambersburg PA
CBHW041101070526
44579CB00003B/37